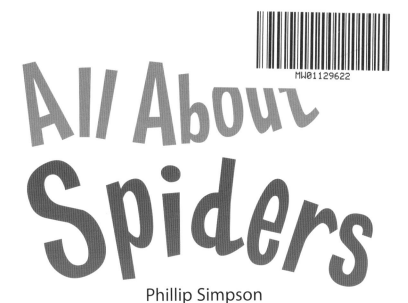

All About Spiders

Phillip Simpson

Contents

What Are Spiders?

Spiders are animals.
They are found in many different places all over the world.

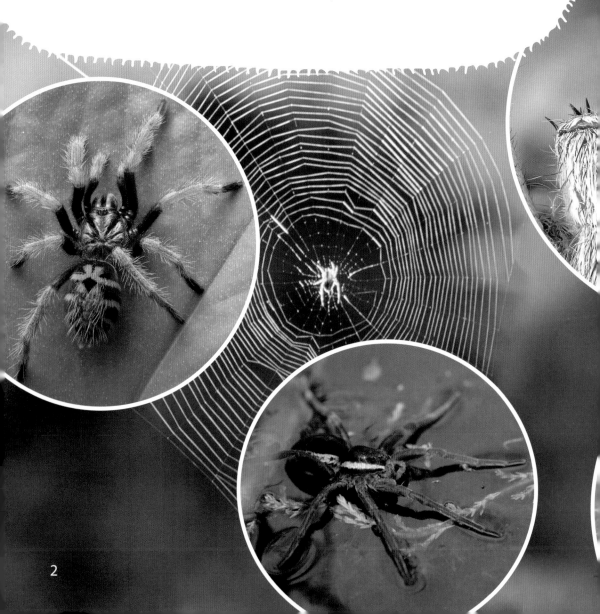

Spiders live in deserts, mountains, and even in water. The only place spiders do not live is in Antarctica.

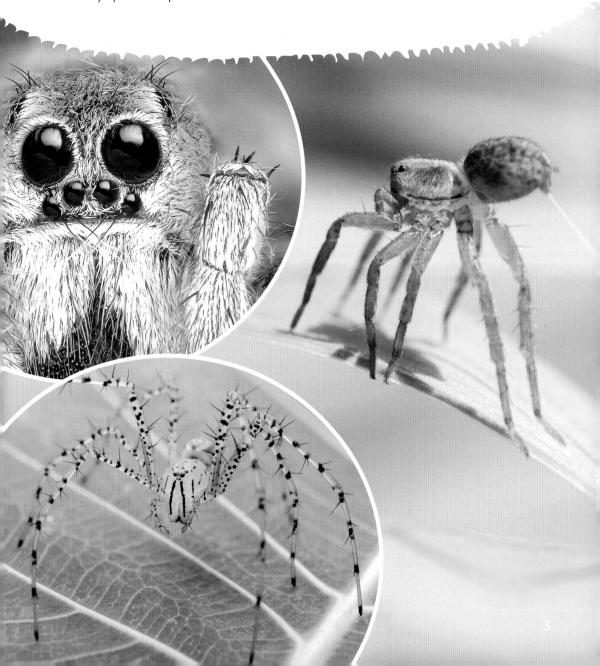

The Parts of a Spider

A spider has two main body parts:
a front part and a rear part.

On the front part of a spider's body
there are eyes, a mouth, and **fangs**.
A spider also has eight long legs
on this part of its body.
The legs are covered with tiny hairs
that help the spider to cling to walls and ceilings.

The rear part of the spider is called the abdomen.
At the end of the abdomen is the **spinneret**.
A spider spins silk from the spinneret to make its web.

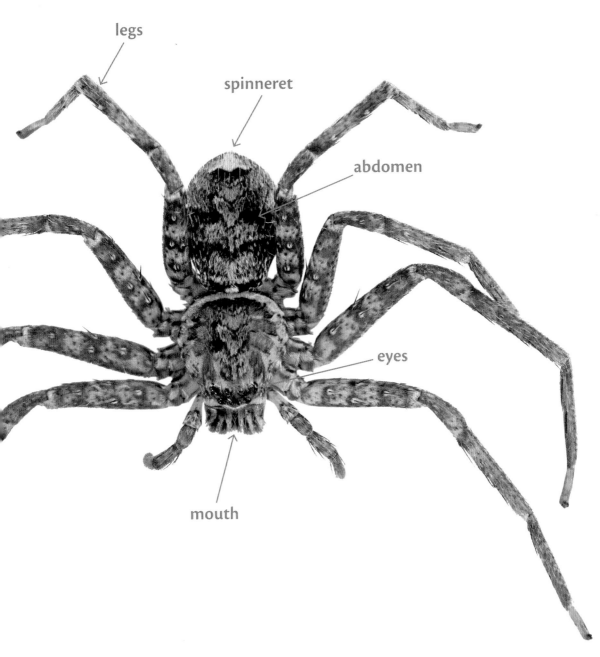

legs

spinneret

abdomen

eyes

mouth

What Spiders Eat

Most spiders eat insects.
Larger spiders also eat small frogs, lizards,
fish, mice, and even birds!

A spider has two big fangs filled with venom.

fangs

Some spiders even eat other spiders.
Spiders have fangs that they use to bite their prey.
The **venom** in their fangs stops the prey from moving.

A Spider's Web

Spiders use their silk to make webs.
The silk is like a clear, sticky thread.
A spider's web is easy to see after it has been raining.
The raindrops make the web **glisten**.

Spiderwebs can be all shapes and sizes.
Some spiders spin large, round webs.
They spread their web between two tree branches
to catch insects.

A spider does not get caught in its own sticky web, though.
It makes a special kind of oil to cover its legs.

Different Kinds of Spiders

There are many different kinds of spiders around the world. Some spiders are huge and others are very small.

The smallest spider in the world is called the Patu Marplesi. This spider is tiny. It is about the size of a period.

This photograph of the tiny Patu Marplesi spider has been enlarged to show its features.

The biggest spider in the world
is the male Goliath Bird-eating Spider.
This spider is as large as a dinner plate.
The Goliath Bird-eating Spider lives longer than most spiders.
It can live for ten years.
Most spiders live for only one or two years.

Hairy Spiders

The hairiest spider in the world is the Tarantula Spider. The Tarantula Spider uses the hairs on its body to **protect** itself.

These hairs are very sharp. They are like little darts.
When the spider is in danger,
it uses its back legs to throw these hairs at a **predator**.

Colorful Spiders

One of the most colorful spiders is the male Peacock Spider. It has bright colors all over its body.

The Happy Face Spider has colors
on the rear part of its body
that look like a smiling face.

Water Spiders

The Water Spider is found all over the world.
It usually lives in ponds or streams.

The Water Spider does not breathe underwater, though.
Bubbles of air are trapped in the hairs that cover its body.

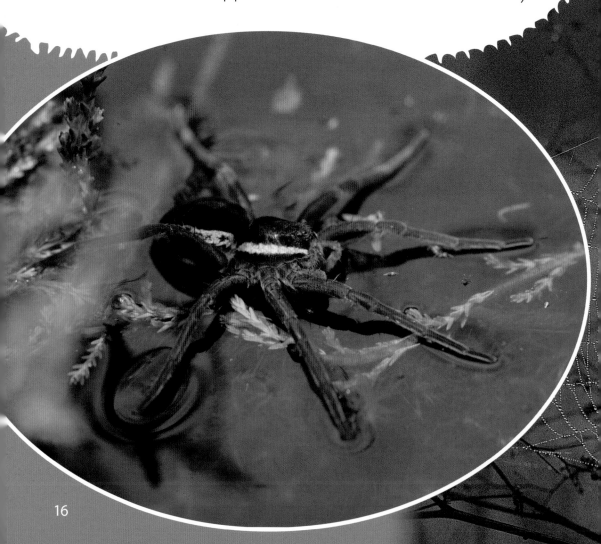

Garden Spiders

Many spiders live in gardens and homes.
The Orb-weaver Spider lives in trees
and builds large, round webs.
It usually waits for its prey in the center of the web.

The Orb-weaver Spider has one of the strongest webs
of all spiders.

The Huntsman Spider

The Huntsman Spider is large and has long legs.
It does not build webs.
The Huntsman Spider can sometimes be found in houses.
This spider does bite, but it is not harmful to people.

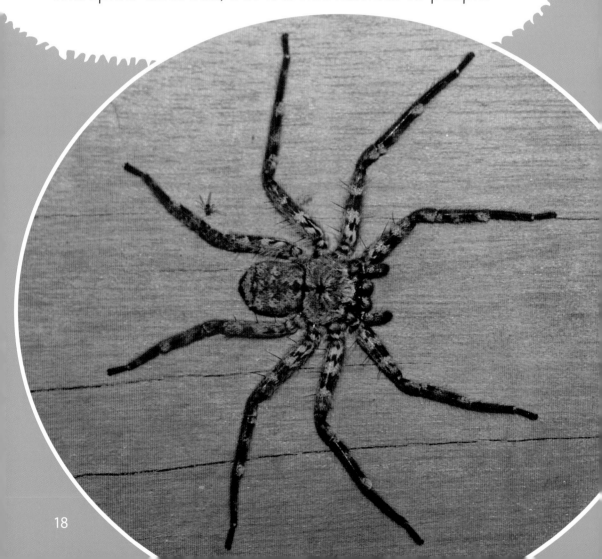

The Wolf Spider

The Wolf Spider is not very big,
but it runs after its prey, like a wolf.
That is why it is called a Wolf Spider.
It is usually grey or brown in color.
The Wolf Spider does not make a web.

The Redback Spider

The Redback Spider is found in most parts
of Australia and New Zealand.
The female spider has a red stripe on its body.
This is a dangerous spider.
The bite of a Redback Spider can make people very sick.

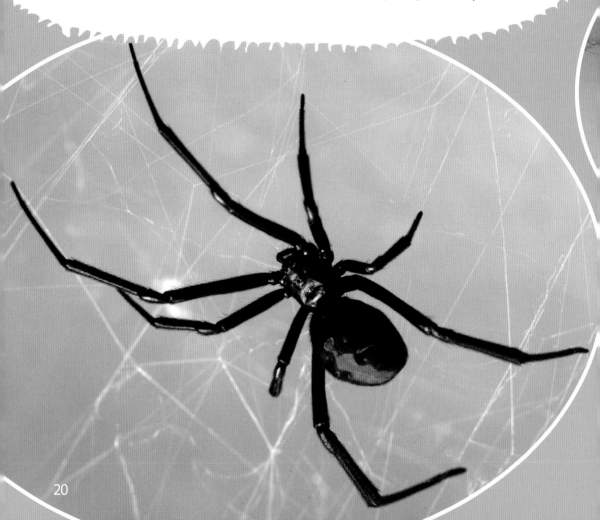

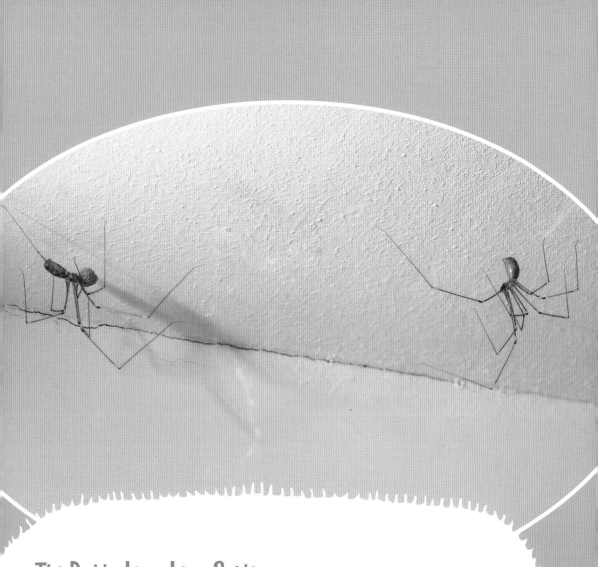

The Daddy-Long-Legs Spider

The Daddy-long-legs Spider is found
in most places in the world.
The Daddy-long-legs Spider does not make a web,
and is often seen inside houses. It is harmless to people.

Spiders and People

Most spiders are not harmful to people.
However, some spiders are dangerous.
Their bites can make people very sick,
or even kill them.

Spiders are special creatures that belong to the animal world.

Glossary

fangs (*noun*)   long, pointed teeth

glisten (verb)   to shine with a sparkling light

predator (*noun*)   an animal that kills and eats other animals

protect (*verb*)   to stop something from being harmed or damaged

spinneret (*noun*)   the part of a spider's body that makes silk

venom (*noun*)   a poisonous substance that can be dangerous to animals and humans

Index